Far From Home

A Young Woman's Journey of Growth, Grit and Discovery

Tanushree Chungi

BookLeaf Publishing

India | USA | UK

Dedication

I dedicate this book to my great-grandfather, Mr. R.M. Joshi, whose legacy continues to inspire me. Though I never had the privilege of meeting him or seeing him in person, the stories of his brilliance and his proficiency in three languages—English, Marathi, and Sanskrit—have profoundly shaped my creative journey. His eloquence as an orator and his mastery over words transcended boundaries, leaving behind a legacy of literary excellence. My poetry is but a fragment of his literary DNA, echoing the passion for language he so gracefully embodied.

I also extend my heartfelt gratitude to my entire family, special mention to my grandmother, my parents, my brother, and my husband. Their unwavering support and encouragement have been the pillars of strength in this poetic endeavor of my life. This book would not have been possible without their love and belief in me.

Preface

This collection of poems is a journey—a tapestry woven with threads of courage, resilience, and discovery. It is the story of a young girl who dared to leave behind the familiar to embrace the unknown in a foreign land. Each poem captures a moment, a feeling, a realization. From the quiet whispers of homesickness to the triumphant echoes of newfound strength, the words are raw and honest. They chronicle her growth as she navigates the delicate balance between holding on and letting go. This collection is a tribute to every heart that beats bravely in an unfamiliar world. May these poems resonate with you, inspire you, and remind you that every journey, no matter how far from home, brings us closer to who we truly are.

Acknowledgements

I am deeply grateful to my family, especially my husband, Rohan Kulkarni, whose unwavering encouragement and daily reminders kept the little poet in me alive. His constant motivation and heartfelt appreciation have been instrumental in bringing this book to life.

I also extend my gratitude to everyone who has directly or indirectly inspired my journey as a writer. A special thanks to *Shark Tank India, Season 4*, for featuring Book leaf Publishing's pitch and for the *21 Days Poetry Challenge*, which reignited my passion for poetry.

1. Far From Home

Far from home, She is far from home,
Bright side of which is, she will learn to live alone,
She will miss the warm hugs and the caring tone,
She will wonder how quickly she has grown.

A new country, a new house, a new job is here,
Her country, Her home & her people is what she wishes
to be near,
She misses the anger and the loud cheer,
Feels like it was yesterday, that she was with her near
and dear.

Education and career has brought her away from home,
Far from home, she is far from home,
This feeling is new and less known,
In this life, she is just a queen looking for her throne.!

2. Surrounded But Alone

Surrounded But Alone
Like the raindrops in the rain,
We are surrounded but alone,
Even with all the experiences of love, pain and gain,
We are surrounded but alone.

Alone we have come, alone we shall go,
In between is all the magic, a pompous show!
Surrounded by people we love, little do we know,
Time never stops, we tend to grow.

We surround ourselves with desires and ambitions,
Life becomes a movie with no intermission,
We get struck with permissions and submissions,
Life keeps changing its definition.

As we age, there is a decrease in our pace and rage,
We start to keep ourselves surrounded at every stage,
But raindrops hit the ground alone,
Surrounded for a long time, but still alone.!

3. Heart on her Sleeve

Tears roll down her eyes, her smile gets too wide,
All her emotions are hard to hide,
She wears her heart on her sleeve,
Dreams with kindness, she wishes to achieve.

She is never scared to share her warmth,
Feelings and sentiments clearly put forth,
She wears her heart on her sleeve,
Believes and does not deceive.!

She is vulnerable, because she is an open book,
Her empathy will make you crave for a closer look,
She wears her heart on her sleeve,
Once you enter her world, it is hard to leave.

4. Journey

Eyes filled with tears and a heart so heavy
There she was standing and making her way through
airport security
She waved and waved to her parents across the airport
door
The stomach wrenching feeling kept soar

There she was, all ready to board the flight,
She kept telling herself , she was doing everything right,
The first international flight of her life took off,
She could feel everything around her scoff.

She cried through the journey and held on to her phone,
Her mom and dad did the same at home,
The girl kept looking at the phone to look at a photo of
her parents,
The parents kept looking at the phone for flight
clearance

Air hostess watched her cry and gaze at them with

fright,
She cried so much and slept through the night,
She did not know how to enjoy a flight,
The destination was almost here ,she had to hang in
tight.

5. Destination via Transit Point

As the flight zoomed through the transit point,
She bravely hopped on to a bigger flight,
Her confidence spurt, the journey was reaching a
turning point,
With memories galore, here she was, the destination was
in sight.

A new country, a new life, everything looked shiny,
The whole world looked huge to her, she felt tiny,
The destination was cold, ground covered with snow,
Her eyes were tired from the sobbing, her face had no
glow

She was picked up from the airport by distant family,
Her hands clutched her phone tight, her surroundings all
uncanny
She then mustered some hope and picked up her phone
Her ears yearned to listen to her parents loving tone

Her mom picked the phone and uttered her name,
Ahh , it felt like her mom had re-ignited the flame,
Holding back tears in her eyes, with a shaky voice she
said,
I have reached mom and dad, look how much your
daughters wings have spread.!

6. International Student

Now she was a student again,
The university had so much to offer,
The library, the classes, the beauty of the campus , so
much to gain,
All clean, all pretty, so many new things in front of her.

She learnt to live a life as a strong independent student,
Courses and homework were her priority,
Her friends and roommates always said she was prudent,
She had now realized now she is the sole authority

Days passed, she worked on campus to pay her bills,
Soon she gained the money managing skills,
She made great friends along the way,
They were her strength in the days of dismay

She was living a life that she never knew she could
Her heart always yearned for her parents and her hood
Some nights were sad and she sobbed herself to sleep

She was homesick of course, her grit was what she was
learning to keep.

9

7. Hope, Faith and Pandemic

Hope is defined as attitude full of optimism & desire,
Faith is the trust or the confidence that fuels our inner
fire,
You hope that the best is yet to come,
You have faith that everything is good and there is no
glum.

Ah.! Our girl had completed a year in the university
The pandemic slowly creeped in, students watched with
a blanket of fear,
The students were away from home, this diseases did not
consider any diversity,
They looked at the statistics and prayed for everyone's
near and dear.

Trapped at home, friendship grew deep
They learnt to co-exist with chores and schedules
The courses were now online, their faith had an impaired
leap
Then came vaccines, that smoothened the hope at

various levels

She would speak to her parents back home thrice a day,
She would give them a million instructions on how to
face these times
They did the same, exclaimed that life is not always grass
,there is a bit of hay,
Both hope and faith had seen a fall, but showed
perseverance to make climbs.

8. Fate and Job Search

"Oh, too bad.! This is my fate!", is something people say,
When things do not go their way,
It is said, to make situations better and less awry,
The blame on fate is mostly accompanied with a sigh.!

Now, was the time the school was coming to an end,
Her safety net almost depleting, here was another
learning curve
She honed her skills, and followed all job market trend,
She calculated all her moves, did not want to swerve

Soon there came an opportunity her way,
Her preparation had a lot of dedication, she wanted to
stand out in a mob,
Trying hard to keep the stress at bay.
She aced the interview and had landed the job.

9. Level Up

Now the level was up, she was no more a student at
school,
She was in a new city, the weather here was not so cool,
There was a lot of sun and she was closer to the beach,
Her goals now seemed within reach.

She soon started working for the company,
She built a small home and her roommate was her best
accompany,
She started paying her bills and made her parents proud,
Oh their little girl, now stood tall in a crowd.

This level in her life was both good and bad,
All she wanted to do was pay the education loan and go
home,
But, the week and the weekends did not cease to add,
Although tuned into her new life, there was one piece of
her heart always missed home

10. Beach- A Happy Place

A happy place, can be a location with address,
Or it can just be state of mind that helps you smile in
distress,
It can be a room where you express,
Or it can just be a corner where you feel a little less
stress.

The beach was her happy place,
She would go to one every weekend,
Sitting there, she watched the waves and felt a safe
space,
She loved the wind, the sand, the water and its deep-end.

She believed everyone needs to find their happy place &
relish,
It will provide them moments they can cherish,
A happy place might keep changing but it will not
perish,
A Happy Place is a real thing & not just a fetish.!

11. Self Love

Self love is not a lesson you master in a time frame,
It is the little silent moments of appreciation or acclaim,
Start off by saying good things about yourself loud,
Feel content and your smile will be the brightest in a
crowd.

You need to believe in yourself and trust your abilities,
You and only you are aware of your capabilities,
Increase the win and reduce the losing probabilities,
Learn from your losses, enjoy the wining activities.

12. Routine

Now there was a routine in her life,
Work, home, grocery and deadlines all in her stride,
There were now some low and some high tides,
Her horizons now were open and knew no ties.

She did her work work on the weekdays
Her adulting chores on the weekends
Her routine did not follow a unique way
Her roommate was confidant, their bond had a deep-end.

Soon her parents realized ,now she was in a routine,
She has now turning into a machine,
They proposed a wedding alliance,
And there it was, she thought it was a pact of
compliance.

13. Husband Hunt

Oh the marriage alliance,
She was asked her preference and her likes,
She answered all the questions without any non
compliance,
She filled bio pages of marriage portals with hobbies and
dislikes.

Her heart did yearn for her man,
She wanted to meet him and hold his hand,
She knew he would make her strong and she trusted in
god's plan,
She read through various bio's, some sweet, some
courageous and some filled with demand.

Five months passed and her parents started feeling the
peer pressure,
She kept her faith in her own little fairy tale,
She believed in arranged marriages and love without
measure,
The universe was preparing her with attention to detail

She then spoke to a guy over the phone,
It seemed like someone she had always known,
She spoke for an hour straight with a complete stranger,
Completely unaware that this call will change her.!

14. Her Guy

She met her witty guy in a small hotel called wittle inn,
He was kind and cute, sometimes would easily give in,
His sense of humor is his jewel,
He is sensitive and sometimes like to dwell

She felt like she had known him from a really long time,
She could talk to him about anything from comedy to
crime,
She often said to him "You love to eat.! and so do I,
I found my shoulder that will help me when I cry.! "

She found her guy, who she can laugh with,
She found her guy, here she was breaking a myth.!

15. A Beginning

A decision that will mark a beginning,
A connection that has bought a lot of grinning
Yes, an agreement that is blessed by families,
An accord to stay happy even during anomalies,

Studious girl has met her match,
The boy is honest, she has found her catch,
The road ahead will not be easy,
Life is tough sometimes, not always rosy.

Sensitive girl has found her man,
He is chivalrous and kind, always has a plan,
Trust and Friendship is what they valued,
Behaviors and quirks can be reviewed,

She was going to be hitched.!
Her comfort zone was going to be switched,
Here she was looking at a new phase,
With Folded hands and a hopeful gaze.

16. Her Feelings

Her friends asked her- how do you feel?
Now that she is getting married, making a move, striking
a deal.!
She said I do not know what I feel,
Life is not as easy as a 30 second Instagram reel.

Yes, she was scared , she will now be sharing her life
Her home, her zone, her heart and her love,
Now, there will be a new person who will be her priority,
It would take her a while to understand that only
counting herself is no more a majority.

A whole new family will be added to her prayer list,
She needs to strike a balance, without a major twist,
She was anxious about this new phase,
She had never been on this side of the race.

But there was a little courage that sprouted from his
love,
She assured herself, they have a blessing from above.

17. Transition Phase

Soon she was married with blessings and positivity
galore,
She entered a new city, a new house with a whole new
family to own,
The little girl who was far from home, realized life has so
much in store,
Here she was with less of known and a lot of unknown.

His love was her constant support,
Her transition from a girl to a wife was short,
She impressed the new family and won many hearts,
She did great, straight A's on all her behavior charts.

Soon they had to come back leaving the family home,
They held hands and boarded the plane,
The girl was far from home again,
But this time, there was no loss only a gain.!

18. Celebration Trip

Far ahead at the end of her line of sight,
The ocean meets the sky without any fright,
The waves have so much chaos and so do the tides,
So much energy powering the boat rides.

Amidst the mayhem, there is a lot of calm
The clear water, the humid wind are a perfect charm,
Far from home, to mark a beginning of a new life,
Some love, some faith, some learning and the transition
to a wife.

19. Quiet Learning

Motivation can be temporary, discipline is what makes it
permanent,
A constant source of strength shall keep your goals
pertinent,
Find the source of your strength,
A song, A book a person or a thought, a support for an
infinite length.

Somethings are not in your control,
Learn to look at life as a whole,
Sometimes chose to impress your soul,
If life is a movie, you are always in the lead role.

20. Finish Lines

We want so much in life, we do not know when to stop,
We keep running towards finish lines that do not cease
to drop,
She started a journey away from home, gravitating
towards the unknown,
Made her parents proud, and paved her path on her own.

The little girl that sobbed in the airport, learned to smile,
She realized that there is no finish line,
Her journey far from from home, bought her closer to
herself mile by mile,
She learnt that life is meant to be change by design.

Completing a degree was never the finish line,
Joining a company to work was never the finish line,
Working and adulting was not the finish line,
Getting married is never a finish line.!

21. You

Far from home means close to yourself,
The strength you get from yourself is the most powerful,
A journey that started out with tears, has now bought
her closer to herself,
With highs and lows, the journey has been fruitful.

Self worth, confidence, respect and kindness are just the
byproducts,
You learn to look within, learn to listen and learn to
grow,
Being assertive and responsive teaches you to avoid
misconducts,
There is a lot of polishing required to bring out that
glow.

Be it silent moments of praise or acclaims,
You learn to center yourself, leant to look at life as a
series of frames,
Every frame unique filled with a different learning and in
vivid colors,

Every situation pushing you closer to yourself than the others.

You have the potential to be great and successful,
Start by believing in yourself and that is plentiful,
You need to back yourself , learn to get up after a fall,
Fight your battles with might, be it the big ones or the small.

www.ingramcontent.com/pod-product-compliance
Lightning Source LLC
LaVergne TN
LVHW021330200726
843509LV00014B/2469